The
Reckless Sleeper

The
Reckless Sleeper

HAIDEE KRUGER

First published in 2012 by Modjaji Books PTY Ltd
P O Box 385, Athlone, 7760, South Africa
modjaji.books@gmail.com
http://modjaji.book.co.za
www.modjajibooks.co.za

ISBN 978-1-920590-31-4

Cover design: Life is Awesome Design Studio
Book design: Life is Awesome Design Studio
Printed and bound by Mega Digital, Cape Town
Set in Palatino

Earlier versions of some of these poems have been
published in the following journals and on the following
websites: *Big Bridge, Botsotso, The Common, Green
Dragon, Litnet, New Coin, New Contrast, Ons Klyntji,
Red Peter.*

The financial contribution of the Office of the Dean:
Faculty of Humanities, North-West University (Vaal Triangle
Campus) towards the publication of this book is gratefully
acknowledged.

For Jan-Louis, Anja,
Tristan and Luka

Contents

Endings

Beginnings

Home/sick

Endings

the end

apocalypse is the first thing after   after
a landslide of red   dreams of black crêpe &   broken glass
a lifetime of nuclear waiting to happen

today i hide while the sky melts like rubber   like a guy fawkes ode
with tomorrow cross-stitched between my legs   sap dripping into my shoes
how else to bleach out afternoons of petrol   strychnine &   rapists on hot tar

always a taste for tightness you had &
me shopping for boys who push my panic buttons
who thought who   thought this

finally after   after
years of keeping still to escape
the horseman and his choir of maggots pining for blood

the maid of orleans does a slow minuet
for the unwilling dead

The letter a

It's the shape of it in the stone –
not the skeletons of clichés, the wilted headstones;
not the architectural litanies against loss
orchestrated by light –

it's the shape of it:

stem and stroke, bowl and counter,
graven beginnings and endings,

a memento mori in type.

It comes down to a letter,
really;

all you are is the
a
in
daughter,

even if the cathedral
hopes

otherwise.

april again

it's april again
and the sun
has a dangerous tilt

in the back garden
the chrysanthemums
bleed headlines

at night
memory picks my locks

tying the knot

to find the sweet damp knot
of knickers, stomach, tongues,

you need
the chafe of loop over cord,
nylon down legs,
body in body –
bent tautline
underhand slide
into bliss.

however,
once doubled over itself
the seam sets into calloused bight,
forever looped,
spliced,
sutured –

hitched right down
to the bitter end.

nothing like

                                                                    nothing like
red flowering neon poinsettia stains on skin when
it's all supposed to be
                white
                on
                white
carefully composed code covering
soundless safranine cells
sprouting
        below

                                                                    nothing like
loss leaking into the bones
wrapping sepia tendrils around
the spine
                spiking into
                bitter juice shadowing
                synaptic apocalypse
        inside

                                                                    nothing like
postpictureexposure numb while
whitechalked voices etch
black print
                paring
                sucking
                scraping
        down

to immaculate
unconception

the betrayed writer

today
i put your pencil

in my
mouth

it tasted of

another woman's
words

Interval

Pull the chord
taut. Tune tighter,

until we wheeze
the strains of
this asphyxiated
tritone sky.

The string cuts a sudden
cadence, drains the blood
from the day.

Augmented silence falls
to the ground,

exhaling absence
out of tune with itself.

curettage

In a swimmingpoolgreen room
I am
a white starfish on white marble under
a white ceiling freezing into
five points measuring the distance to

dead centre

I leach colourless jelly into
my veins fossilising like dry rivers
until

I fluoresce out in strobes clinging to
the voices, the steel ebbing against my back,
the weight of my
belly

I emerge on
the other side
into rain evaporating off hot tar

I have been cured of
my body

december

i strap a red leather belt around my hips
to fake

where your hands used
to lie,

shutter my skull and
listen to

the way the highveld earth contracts
underfoot.

Writer

I keep my tools
hidden,
until the sun rasps
its black breath over
the suburbs. Only then

do I edge from
my demure murmuring disguise,
carrying my pen like
an axe,
waiting in the underbrush for
the first bloodwarm faces
to appear. I like

to slaughter the meat out
of them, to space
their soft stomachs across
the page, to stretch
their sinews into
stems and curves,

or else
to pull their wet skins tight,
nailing them down around
the white silences
squirming. I never

wash my hands
after – the whimpers dry
to innocent ink under
my nails. And besides,

I keep my tools
hidden.

cradle

so far
i have thrown
words like
        wineglasses
                stones
                        handgrenades
at the head
of god

but today
i will
go out
to collect some instead –
        soft and round like
        churchbells
                pistachio green
                    slippery like
                    fresh eggs
                            filled
                            with sap

i will offer them
to you
as a cradle
to sleep in

For A, four years old this spring

You ask

if we are allowed
to talk about

the deadness of
plum blossoms
in a glass jar

and I have to think
before saying

yes.

Funeral

In this place,

where the body
shatters into
worddust drifting
in a curious quiet hymn of
autumn light humming

I grope against
the grain of time-
worn benches, against
the vaulting sadness, for

a shape that comforts
beyond this skin

but come back with
knotted hands, salt-
sting tongue,
body against body,
breath.

Beginnings

the beginning

the table is
a breath between us
a shiver of a thing
aching

the edges of the room
curl around my wrist
a cuff of blood

glasses echo
my fingers taste the bones
of your head

my mouth is a beggar
under the table
a hunter of slivers
a gasp of shards

somewhere
beyond the din
of crockery and teeth

is a tongue not just
for crumbling
not just
for crumbs

Mermaid song

It's a different element: turbid, electric, saline.
You have to prove your fins
before we can let you in.

A toe to the water is not an option;
there is only full immersion,
scraping away the scales until you're just
the pulse of raw meat baptised in brine.

It's a red tide, a lick of phototactic tongue ebbing,
or a mermaid disappearing into her gills,
depending.

This place aches and aches and aches its fluorescent beat.
You have to prove your fins
before we can let you in.

gravity's girl

been cruising
the past, popping
pink lines and prophecies when

down he comes, oak & iron under
his breath, flooding
black ink & milk like
a warm tongue,   a holy host flexed
into sap & soil,
            a cryptic seed,   a moan,
p r e s s e d
into flesh
ver.te.bra by ver.te.bra

I'm gravity's girl, weighted & wanting
                              More,
a cellular stew speaking
a swell like an ocean,   an everywhere
concertinaed in the cage of my ribs,
        loaded with lead &
the littoral world

I am
eight arms, eight legs,
        belly
a hard beak sharpened by the wind,
        eyes
                    Open.

The way light falls

It's Wednesday and
the sky has
a biblical look
to it, like
a prophet's beard
straggling red over
the horizon. She
picks up her
weight and walks
through the gate,
into the morning.
Her body disappears
but she leaves
tracks in the
mud: an invitation
for hunting. In

the street children
cling to the
pavement while their
mothers unplug themselves
from the day
ahead. The wind
sleeps between buildings.
She watches the
chickens like 3D-mosaics
behind wire, and
wonders about feathered
things and how
to kill them.
She buys a
remote control and

notes the particular
taste of milk
and metal on
her tongue, and
thinks: none of

us understand our
breathing, still we
breathe; still we
remember how a
kiss can turn
you into a
stranger to yourself.
Yes, there is
redemption in this,
she says to
her belly: the
way light falls
on hands here.

bridge

there is a bridge she drives over every morning. approaching it, she undoes
/last night/ her seat belt, switches off the radio, opens the locks /i dreamt an
immersion/, winds down the window. it is a bridge /in you/ that promises
collapse /the way your hands unravel my spine/ every time it comes into view.
there are potholes that look as if they must extend /legs like milk on the sheets
and you inhaling/ all the way through. the concrete barriers /a liquid path/ at
the side, regiments of muscles at attention, have been ripped out, torn away.
the bridge stumbles /swimming/. some have been replaced by twisted strands
of wire, loose stitches /mouth and skin/ keeping it together. below the water
is a dirty simmer /undone by you/. there are vagrants camping on the banks,
welded /leaking/ to the mud. she slows down, concentrates on the mechanics
of maneuvering around the wormholes /falling tongues, a river above, i/. once
complete, the bridge recedes /beggars both/ into the mirror. she clicks her
seatbelt in, switches on the radio /a bloodied shore/, locks the door, winds up
the window.

Ultrasound picture

This
is how you are not
yourself,

    this
    warm beating thing
    burrowed in ultraviolet dusk.

    This
is how you wear
your flesh

    inside out,
    outside in:
    arms through heart,
    body a bulb breathing against dirt.

    This
is how you are

    a carefully knitted skein
    a sunrise of cells brittle

but unafraid
leaning
into.

satellite

the heaviness of words
does not
compare :: the tongue

is not

a belly ::

just a cataract of syllables glued to the horizon like a ribbon of breadcrumbs
words that
only bear repeating
on. ly. bear. re. peat. ing

but
your body is a satellite
between my ribs
your spine is
wordless weight

the belly sighs
its   births
                            its   skin
                                            its   e v e r y t h i n g s

:: no poem will be
as luminous
as this ::

the heaviness of words
does not
compare

No place like home

Autumn
shivers
a chink into
interrupted cupboards.
       Measured by
       still-translucent
       fingerprints,
       I pack
       monstrous monsoons into drawers,
       drape fallen skies on hangers.
              The cellular geometry inside
              demands
              seepage into
              the world, while
                     time
                     clicks
                     her heels
                     in a copper dactyl underfoot,
                     soles
                     photosynthesising serenely.
                            Death
                            by diction
                            is nothing. Therefore.
                                    There is
                                    no place
                                    like home:

                                        the undertow of
                            wings sutured
              breath
        less
   ly
on closet mirrors.

the Body

the Body rearranges
itself around
the other.   points of entry and exit,
embraces.   Embraces.   the
thrill of skin.   density
surrenders to Liquid.   semen, blood,
mucous, milk.   the Body yields to

its double.   it takes One into,
lets One out.   it breathes only
in reflection.   in between,

the Body grows into
the swell of a question mark.   then.
Then.

pain pinballs echoes,
cell to amnesiac cell.   the Past fleshed
unexpectedly.   the Body

is a superconductor, pure
light leaping.   Time pours
out of it, a warm rush of
presentness.   Inhale.   the beating
world.   Exhale.

Again.   Again.
Again.

and after
the Body shrinkwraps
loss, ties it with red ribbons.   the Body
rearranges, leaks, empties
itself of
Itself.   demands to be
mopped up.   staunched,
stoppered.   yes.   Yes.
the Body returns to

the shape of a comma.   a breathless
Pause.

.

It's autumn

and the world
slowly turns itself
upside
down.

Too densely debris'ed below,
too
sparse
above.

Kerning undone,
the soil
teems fat lobes,
composted counters.

The sky is
a pencilbox of picas
punching holes
through
paper;

handfuls of
stems,
strokes,
spurs:

brittle stubble
bruising
a soft belly.

The eye
recoils;

the body
grows unsteady,
without rest.

Yes.
It's autumn and

the world
hesitates in
the space
between.

Milk

for L

It's called milk but really
I feed you
aloe and salt,
>   the deadends of my body swallowed by
>   the dark work of growing,
>>   a void carbonated with black holes, thick with
>>   the places where women drain themselves of themselves,
>>>   liquid shadow in
>>>   negative.

Here is my body.
>   Take it.
>>   Eat it.

This,
and a prayer that
your alchemy will not fail you,
you who are
>   so confident
>>   in your light.

the green snake

for T

you follow
the green snake
through the big world

right up

to where
the outside washes against the gate
in slow waves of tar and leaves
and strangenesses passing by
until

you find it:

an unpredicted fountain shivering with
newness
so shiny   so liquid
so all the time   so there
so
much to touch.

and i say:
sweet boy
sorry
no.
your hands will be cold   you'll be wet   and it's winter
just wait.

so
you let me pick you up and carry you away
through the big world
right back

to where
we started
looking back all the way
to make sure it's
still
there.

and i know
you'll remember this:
the looking   the wanting

and i know it's
the looking   the wanting
i'll remember.

the underground

the man with the concertina
playing psalms while staring at
a poster of madonna nodded
at the money and said
it seems i should learn
how to juggle   &   the blonde
woman with the perfect knees
pulled out split hairs putting
them on her lap to
count and when she couldn't
find any more she split
some with her boyfriend who
was trying to sleep but
couldn't because of the smell
of oranges and the old
man turning the pages of
his book next to him
like a bedroom door shutting
and said i need to
have a baby   &   the mystic
with the hair like the
wing of a crow and
the ayurvedic body oil sang
and smiled but did not
say i need you so
the man with the level
tasting women with nipples black
like olives said find a
cliché and fall in love
with it   &   the boy chewing
his shoelaces looked at the
girl counting the stitches in

her skull and said you'll
be needing both hands to
hold on to reality   &   the
reader holding her book gently
to keep its spine smooth
like a new body said
why keep your tongue in
your mouth?   &   the sleeper with
the ears of a wolf
slumbered without dreaming while   the
child without a mouth said
you are a container for
all this all this all
this all yes i said

Home/sick

Home/sick

Love can be a blanket, here,
not a bulletproof vest.
No dogs bark in the night.
Nobody weeps or screams, though
there is evidence of dreaming,
sieved over the soil in the morning light.
People do not sell cigarettes on pavements.
Nobody gets struck by lightning. The world
wears earmuffs. Glass is enough.

But home is always there,
or here,
or neither here
nor there:
skulking like a sneeze that doesn't come,
a magnetic scar,
a memory of moulting,
an orphaned star.

Gilleleje, Denmark

walking at night in winter

this is the second.
first
inside it,
death undone,
the chin.
the same.

the
is remembered
a
buttoned to
it is not
but.

but.
is a net
molecular gasp
the scabs
unused to
saturating

the body
for dredging:
of an organism without
of streetlights,
absence
the skull.

it was necessary
it is
now

then.
necessary
to imagine.

to imagine
dark shapes
insidious
the street is
lying on the earth
the end of

eyes,
in hedges,
intent, even if
just there,
like limbs at
love.

love.
was then
watching.

there must be, there
something
someone to see.

to see   my hair in the wind,
the trees,   my bones climbing through
my skin,   the sea pouring over
the edge of   the world.

Gilleleje, Denmark

Gift

You open your eyes
to the light that, here,
is always already
there, and say:

Snow.
Horse.
Boat.

You give me
the coordinates of your dreams.

Holsen, Norway

Oh

Oh,
let me be worthy
to be called yours,

to be lost
and found

by your
mouth.

Swansea, Wales

The reckless sleeper

Time,

I thought.

Coffeed & inked. Light scarred against mirrors while she practised the world on paper. Kafka crumbling against the comfort of spoons, scarves, skin.

Time,

I thought.

Desire watercoloured, worn like a locket. Who dares not to speak?

Not to run like a child after a blue pigeon? Not to offer the mouth for eating, not to follow? Who dares not to? Step in, fall through. Kissing crows and candles. Again.

Time,

I thought.

And Leonard wept as she chose the colours of this place:

rhubarb, tea stains, ginger, asphalt, biscuit, scissors, guinness, tongue, memory, bone, canvas, railway, wax, egg, fire.

Time,

I thought.

A reckless sleeper. A puzzle of objects, a guarding blanket. The horror of a blue ribbon. The hollowness of hats. Something to touch.

Time,

I thought.

Walking through revolving doors.

The Tate Modern/Starbucks, London

Evening walk

At dusk, we walk through the dank slush of new life straining
through the sieve of birch, raspberry, mushroom;
rotting stubble blossoming bruises underfoot.

At the top of the path there is the sea, and people enjambed with the light;
their faces turned to the sun lying on the horizon like an afterbirth.

Above an aeroplane scalpels the cooling sky in two,
on its way towards or away from home.

Gilleleje, Denmark

Life stains everything

Inside the blue room, life
stains everything. Outside

there are Tarot cards to be read and
ammonites to be deflowered while
people button and unbutton one another in passing,

much unlike stones in a river. As elsewhere, the sun
does not come out and
few trees consider how they seldom consider how
important it is to know how to weave.

Disrespectfully I must decline this day.
There are too many clouds that are
impossible to unthink. Still,

yarn becomes yearn
with just a little extra ink.

Edinburgh Castle, Edinburgh

Home, older

As my skull swells into
brittle pericarp and
my bones turn soft
like sponge I
learn better how to leave
my sentences
delicate and open
like cottonseed clinging to stalks
in winter light.

Makhado, South Africa

homecoming

is a flock of birds
suddenly spattering across the sky,
girls puzzled like pomegranates and
a skyline that makes
you weep

Poem for my father

Today I am my father, lining
up brown paper, scissors, plastic, tape,
his hands dappled origami birds over
the ribcages of the unlived year, or else
exorcising wrinkles in a halo of steam and crisp cotton,
his face a furrow brimming with silent seeds.

I never thought these things wings, and yet,
today I cut the shapes we learn without knowing.
A corner is a treacherous thing –
the angle should be
just so –
but it is nothing against a spine.
You want it planed and sleek but not
too taut, a living
supple string, much like the faultline that runs down the leg,
fabric that echoes skin in secret places.

Time folds. Today I see:
inside the geometries of my father
is tucked the softest rumple of things, feathering.

Other Poetry Titles by Modjaji Books

Fourth Child
by **Megan Hall**

Life in Translation
by **Azila Talit Reisenberger**

Please, Take Photographs
by **Sindiwe Magona**

Burnt Offering
by **Joan Metelerkamp**

Strange Fruit
by **Helen Moffett**

Oleander
by **Fiona Zerbst**

The Everyday Wife
by **Phillippa Yaa de Villiers**

missing
by **Beverly Rycroft**

These are the lies I told you
by **Kerry Hammerton**

Conduit
by **Sarah Frost**

The Suitable Girl
by **Michelle McGrane**

Piece Work
by **Ingrid Andersen**

Difficult Gifts
by **Dawn Garisch**

Woman Unfolding
by **Jenna Mervis**

removing
by **Melissa Butler**

At least the Duck Survived
by **Margaret Clough**

Bare & Breaking
by **Karin Schimke**

www.modjajibooks.co.za